Reading And Speaking English By Sound

by

Nate Green, Sr.

RoseDog ❧ Books
PITTSBURGH, PENNSYLVANIA 15238

RoseDog Books
585 Alpha Drive, Suite 103
Pittsburgh, PA 15238
Visit our website at www.rosedogbookstore.com

ISBN: 978-1-6442-6574-1
eISBN: 978-1-6442-6597-0

Contents

    The Long Sound of "Aa"
    The Short Sound of "Aa"
    Self-Test

    The Long Sound of "Bb"
    The Short Sound of "Bb"
    Self-Test

    The Long Sound of "Cc"
    The Short Sound of "Cc"
    Self-Test

    The Long Sound of "Dd"
    The Short Sound of "Dd"
    Self-Test

    The Long Sound of "Ee"
    The Short Sound of "Ee"
    Self-Test

    The Long Sound of "Ff"
    The Short Sound of "Ff"
    Self-Test

    The Long Sound of "Gg"
    The Short Sound of "Gg"
    Self-Test

Contents

Contents

Contents

Introduction

This book is a non-traditional way to read and speak English by sound. Traditionally, vowels (a, e, i, o, u, and sometimes y) are the only letters in the alphabet that have long and short sounds. In this book, we give all 26 letters of the alphabet a long and short sound. This makes it easier to pronounce, remember, and identify words. Those who use this book should learn the long and short sounds of each letter in the alphabet. When a person comes to a word they can not pronounce, they should put the sounds of each letter together to help pronounce the word. This book is for all ages.

Lesson 1:
The Long and Short Sounds of "Aa"

To pronounce the long "Aa" sound:
1. Place tongue against the middle of bottom teeth
2. Spread lips apart (lips in smiling position)
3. Pronounce by slightly opening mouth
4. Ending position of tongue is at bottom of lower teeth

Words with the long "Aa" sound:
ape, April, age, able, ace, page, made, rate, tape, day

To pronounce the short "Aa" sound:
1. Place tongue against the middle of lower teeth
2. Pronounce by slightly opening mouth
3. Ending position of tongue is at bottom of lower teeth

Words with the short "Aa" sound:
all, also, art, are, arm, tall, hat, bat, cat, cap

Self-Test:
1. Name the 4 steps to pronounce the long "Aa" sound.
2. Name 10 words with the long "Aa" sound.
3. Name the 3 steps to pronounce the short "Aa" sound.
4. Name 10 words with the short "Aa" sound.

Lesson 2:
The Long and Short Sounds of "Bb"

To pronounce the long "Bb" sound:
1. Place tongue against the middle of bottom teeth
2. Place lips together
3. Fold lips inward
4. Pronounce by slightly opening mouth
5. Ending position of tongue is at bottom of lower teeth

Words with the long "Bb" sound:
beat, bee, be, beef, beast, beach

To pronounce the short "Bb" sound:
1. Place tongue against the middle of bottom teeth
2. Place lips together
3. Fold lips inward
4. Pronounce by slightly opening mouth
5. Ending position of tongue is located at bottom of lower teeth

Words with the short "Bb" sound:
ball, by, but, boy, bay, bank, bug, bird, bite, big

Self-Test:
1. Name the 5 steps to pronounce the long "Bb" sound.
2. Name 6 words with the long "Bb" sound.
3. Name the 5 steps to pronounce the short" Bb" sound.
4. Name 10 words with the short "Bb" sound.

Lesson 3:
The Long and Short Sounds of "Cc"

To pronounce the long "Cc" sound:

1. Place tongue near top of lower teeth
2. Pronounce by slightly opening mouth
3. Spread lips apart (lips in smiling position)
4. Ending position of tongue is at bottom of lower teeth

Words with the long "Cc" sound:

cent, cell, censor, census, city, ceiling, cease

To pronounce the short "Cc" sound:

1. Place tongue near top of lower teeth
2. Pronounce by slightly opening mouth
3. Ending position of tongue is at bottom of mouth

Words with the short "Cc" sound:

cap, cook, cow, cake, car, cat, can coat, call, cold

Self-Test:

1. Name the 4 steps to pronounce the long "Cc" sound.
2. Name 7 words with the long "Cc" sound.
3. Name the 3 steps to pronounce the short "Cc" sound.
4. Name 10 words with the short "Cc" sound.

Lesson 4:
The Long and Short Sounds of "Dd"

To pronounce the long "Dd" sound:
1. Place tongue at top of mouth near rear of top teeth
2. Spread lips slightly apart (lips in smiling position)
3. Pronounce by slightly opening mouth
4. Ending position of tongue is at bottom of lower teeth

Words with the long "Dd" sound:
deed, deep, December, decal, defect, decay, deodorant, decent

To pronounce the short "Dd" sound:
1. Place tongue at top of mouth near rear of top teeth
2. Pronounce by slightly opening mouth
3. Ending position of tongue is at bottom of lower teeth

Words with the short "Dd" sound:
dog, dig, dad, doll, door, dock, dear, dark, date, did

Self-Test:
1. Name the 4 steps to pronounce the long "Dd" sound.
2. Name 8 words with the long "Dd" sound.
3. Name the 3 steps to pronounce the short "Dd" sound.
4. Name 10 words with the short "Dd" sound.

Lesson 5:
The Long and Short Sounds of "Ee"

To pronounce the long "Ee" sound:
1. Place tongue near top of bottom teeth
2. Spread lips slightly apart (lips in smiling position)
3. Pronounce by slightly opening mouth
4. Ending position of tongue is at bottom of lower teeth

Words with the long "Ee" sound:
eve, we, even, easy, ego, east, eat, ease, Eli, he

"Yy" sometimes as the long sound of "Ee."
baby, Tommy, sunny, funny, only, Tony, daddy, pony, lady, party

To pronounce the short "Ee" sound:
1. Place tongue near top of bottom teeth
2. Pronounce by slightly opening mouth
3. Ending position of tongue is at bottom of mouth

Words with the short "Ee" sound:
ear, egg, Ed, elf, earth, education, Eddie, early, earn, echo

Self-Test:
1. Name the 4 steps to pronounce the long "Ee" sound.
2. Name 10 words with the long "Ee" sound.
3. Name the 3 steps to pronounce the short "Ee" sound.
4. Name 10 words with the short "Ee" sound.
5. Name 10 words with "Yy" pronounced as the long "Ee" sound.

Lesson 6:
The Long and Short Sounds of "Ff"

To pronounce the long "Ff" sound:
1. Place tongue against the middle of bottom teeth
2. Pronounce by folding bottom lip over lower teeth
3. Open mouth slightly
4. Place top teeth on bottom lip briefly
5. Ending position of tongue is at middle of lower teeth (step-1)

Words with the long "Ff" sound:
elf, deaf, hefty, self, Jeff, left

To pronounce the short "Ff" sound:
1. Place tongue against the middle of bottom teeth
2. Pronounce by folding bottom lip over lower teeth
3. Place top teeth on bottom lip briefly
4. Open mouth slightly
5. Ending position of tongue is at middle of lower teeth

Words with the short "Ff" sound:
for, fat, far, fall, fan, fast, flat, fix, find, fly

Self-Test:
1. Name the 5 steps to pronounce the long "Ff" sound.
2. Name 6 words with the long "Ff" sound.
3. Name the 5 steps to pronounce the short "Ff" sound.
4. Name 10 words with the short "Ff" sound.

Lesson 7:
The Long and Short Sounds of "Gg"

To pronounce the long "Gg" sound:
1. Place tongue against the middle of lower teeth
2. Bring top and bottom teeth together
3. Pronounce by slightly opening mouth
4. Slightly spread lip apart (lips in smiling position)
5. Ending position of tongue is at bottom of lower teeth

Words with the long "Gg" sound:
gene, Gina, Gino, geology, genus, genie, biology, allergy, energy, analogy

To pronounce the short "Gg" sound:
1. Place tongue against the middle of lower teeth
2. Pronounce by slightly opening mouth
3. Ending position of tongue is at bottom of lower teeth

Words with the short "Gg" sound:
good, get, give, gum, guy, go, gave, gas, game, grow

Self-Test:
1. Name the 5 steps to pronounce the long "Gg" sound.
2. Name 10 words with the long "Gg" sound.
3. Name the 3 steps to pronounce the short "Gg" sound.
4. Name 10 words with the short "Gg" sound.

Lesson 8:
The Long and Short Sounds of "Hh"

To pronounce the long "Hh" sound:
1. Place tongue against the middle of the lower teeth
2. Pronounce by slightly opening mouth
3. Slightly spread lips apart (lips in smiling position)
4. Bring teeth together
5. Separate teeth
6. Ending position of tongue is at bottom of lower teeth

Abbreviations with the long "Hh" sound:
PhD, Hq, Hs, HR, Ph

To pronounce the short "Hh" sound:
1. Place tongue against the middle of lower teeth
2. Pronounce by slightly opening mouth
3. Ending position of tongue is at bottom of lower teeth

Words with the short "Hh" sound:
hill, had, hat, her, he, hay, how, hit, have, him

Self-Test:
1. Name the 6 steps to pronounce the long "Hh" sound.
2. Name 5 abbreviations with the long "Hh" sound.
3. Name the 3 steps to pronounce the short "Hh" sound.
4. Name 10 words with the short "Hh" sound.

Lesson 9:
The Long and Short Sounds of "Ii"

To pronounce the long "Ii" sound:
1. Place tongue against the middle of lower teeth
2. Pronounce by slightly opening mouth
3. Ending position of tongue is at bottom of lower teeth

Words with the long "Ii" sound:
pie, ice, ideal, idle, hi, high, ivy, item, ivory, tie

"Yy" sometimes as the long sound of "Ii:"
cry, by, try, buy, fly, my, fry, spy, guy, dry

To pronounce the short "Ii" sound:
1. Place tongue against the middle of lower teeth
2. Pronounce by slightly opening mouth
3. Ending position of tongue is at bottom of mouth

Words with the short "Ii" sound:
if, it, hit, pit, dig, in, pick, pig, fit, kick

Self-Test:
1. Name the 3 steps to pronounce the long "Ii" sound.
2. Name 10 words with the long "Ii" sound.
3. Name the 3 steps to pronounce the short "Ii" sound.
4. Name 10 words with the short "Ii" sound.
5. Name 10 words with "Yy" sometimes as the long sound of "Ii:"

Lesson 10:
The Long and Short Sounds of "Jj"

To pronounce the long "Jj" sound:
1. Place tongue against the middle of bottom teeth
2. Place top and bottom teeth together
3. Pronounce by slightly opening mouth
4. Separate teeth
5. Spread lips apart (lips in smiling position)
6. Ending position of tongue is at bottom of lower teeth

Words with the long "Jj" sound:
Jake, Jay, Jade, Jacob

To pronounce the short "Jj" sound:
1. Place tongue against the middle of bottom teeth
2. Place top and bottom teeth together
3. Pronounce by slightly opening mouth
4. Ending position of tongue is at bottom of lower teeth

Words with the short "Jj" sound:
June, Jack, jug, job, joy, Joe, jam, jail, James, jog

Self-Test:
1. Name the 6 steps to pronounce the long "Jj" sound.
2. Name 4 words with the long "Jj" sound.
3. Name the 4 steps to pronounce the short "Jj" sound.
4. Name 10 words with the short "Jj" sound.

Lesson 11:
The Long and Short Sounds of "Kk"

To pronounce the long "Kk" sound:
1. Place tongue against the middle of bottom teeth
2. Pronounce by slightly opening mouth
3. Slightly spread lips apart (lips in smiling position)
4. Ending position of tongue is at bottom of lower teeth

Words with the long "Kk" sound:
Kate, Katie, Kay

To pronounce the short "Kk" sound:
1. Place tongue against the middle of bottom teeth
2. Pronounce by slightly opening mouth
3. Ending position of tongue is at bottom of lower teeth

Words with the short "Kk" sound:
kid, kick, key, kin, kite, kind, keep, kit, kill, king

Self-Test:
1. Name the 4 steps to pronounce the long "Kk" sound.
2. Name 3 words with the long "Kk" sound.
3. Name the 3 steps to pronounce the short "Kk" sound.
4. Name 10 words with the short "Kk" sound.

Lesson 12:
The Long and Short Sounds of "Ll"

To pronounce the long "Ll" sound:
1. Place tongue against the middle of bottom teeth
2. Pronounce by slightly opening mouth
3. Slightly spread lips apart (lips in smiling position)
4. Rotate tongue to bottom of lower teeth
5. Next, rotate tongue to the top of mouth
6. Finally, rotate tongue to the bottom of lower teeth
7. Ending position of tongue is at bottom of lower teeth

Words with the long "Ll" sound:
tell, tail, nail, mail, shell, jail, snail, bail, gel, fell,

To pronounce the short "Ll" sound:
1. Place tongue at the middle of bottom teeth
2. Rotate tongue to top of mouth
3. Pronounce by slightly opening mouth
4. Finally, rotate tongue to the bottom of lower teeth
5. Ending position of tongue is at bottom of lower teeth

Words with the short "Ll" sound:
like, leg, law, look, love, lot, land, live, low, lad

Self-Test:
1. Name the 7 steps to pronounce the long "Ll" sound.
2. Name 10 words with the long "Ll" sound.
3. Name the 5 steps to pronounce the short "Ll" sound.
4. Name 10 words with the short "Ll" sound.

Lesson 13:
The Long and Short Sounds of "Mm"

To pronounce the long "Mm" sound:
1. Place tongue against the middle of the bottom teeth
2. Pronounce by slightly opening mouth
3. Slightly spread lips apart (lip in smiling position)
4. Bring lips together (sound comes from nose)
5. Ending position of tongue is at bottom of lower teeth

Words with the long "Mm" sound:
limb, film, him, dim, Kim, rim, gym, Tim, Jim, gem

To pronounce the short "Mm" sound:
1. Place tongue against the middle of bottom teeth
2. Pronounce by slightly opening mouth
3. Ending position of tongue is at bottom of mouth

Words with the short "Mm" sound:
mom, move, must, many, made, make, milk, Mike, mix, man

Self-Test:
1. Name the 5 steps to pronounce the long "Mm" sound.
2. Name 10 words with the long "Mm" sound.
3. Name the 3 steps to pronounce the short "Mm" sound.
4. Name 10 words with the short "Mm" sound.

Lesson 14:
The Long and Short Sounds of "Nn"

To pronounce the long "Nn" sound:
1. Place tongue against the middle of bottom teeth
2. Pronounce by slightly opening mouth
3. Slightly spread lips apart (lips in smiling position)
4. Rotate tongue first to bottom of mouth, next place tongue at top of mouth, and finally place tongue at bottom of lower teeth (sound come from nose)
5. Ending position of tongue is at bottom of lower teeth

Words with the long "Nn" sound:
thin, enjoy, hen, in, win, end, pin, den, invite, entry

To pronounce the short "Nn" sound:
1. Place tongue against bottom of lower teeth
2. Pronounce by slightly opening mouth
3. Spread lips apart (lips in smiling position)
4. Rotate tongue first to top of mouth, next place tongue at bottom of lower teeth
5. Ending position of tongue is at bottom of lower teeth

Words with the short "Nn" sound:
no, neck, next, news, not, note, name, nap, nail, near

Self-Test:
1. Name the 5 steps to pronounce the long "Nn" sound.
2. Name 10 words with the long "Nn" sound.
3. Name the 5 steps to pronounce the short "Nn" sound.
4. Name 10 words with the short "Nn" sound.

Lesson 15:
The Long and Short Sounds of "Oo"

To pronounce the long "Oo" sound:
1. Place tongue against the middle of bottom teeth
2. Pronounce by slightly opening mouth
3. Shape mouth in oval position
4. Ending position of tongue is at bottom of mouth

Words with the long "Oo" sound:
ozone, oral, omit, oak, open, oh, no, radio, go, ocean

To pronounce the short "Oo" sound:
1. Place tongue against the middle of bottom teeth
2. Pronounce by slightly opening mouth
3. Ending position of tongue is at bottom of mouth

Words with the short "Oo" sound:
doll, box, our, out, off, odd, of, ox, or, not

Self-Test:
1. Name the 4 steps to pronounce the long "Oo" sound.
2. Name 10 words with the long "Oo" sound.
3. Name the 3 steps to pronounce the short "Oo" sound.
4. Name 10 words with the short "Oo" sound.

Lesson 16:
The Long and Short Sounds of "Pp"

To pronounce the long "Pp" sound:
1. Place tongue against the middle of bottom teeth
2. Place lips together
3. Pronounce by slightly opening mouth
4. Slightly spread lips apart (lips in smiling position)
5. Ending position of tongue is at bottom of lower teeth

Words with the long "Pp" sound:
peek, peace, peach, peanut, Pete, Peter, pea, piece, peak, peep

To pronounce the short "Pp" sound:
1. Place tongue against the middle of bottom teeth
2. Place lips together
3. Pronounce by slightly opening mouth
4. Ending position of tongue is at bottom of lower teeth

Words with the short "Pp" sound:
pay, pig, play, pat, pan, pop, pack, pick, pot, pull

Self-Test:
1. Name the 5 steps to pronounce the long "Pp" sound.
2. Name 10 words with the long "Pp" sound.
3. Name the 4 steps to pronounce the short "Pp" sound.
4. Name 10 words with the short "Pp" sound.

Lesson 17:
The Long and Short Sounds of "Qq"

To pronounce the long "Qq" sound:
1. Place tongue against the middle of bottom teeth
2. Pronounce by slightly opening mouth
3. Bring lips to a slightly open position (extend lips outward)
4. Ending position of tongue is at bottom of lower teeth

Words and abbreviations with the long "Qq" sound:
barbeque, QB, Q&A, bar-b-q

To pronounce the short "Qq" sound:
1. Place tongue against the middle of bottom teeth
2. Pronounce by slightly opening mouth
3. Bring lips to a slightly open position (extend lips outward)
4. Ending position of tongue is at bottom of lower teeth

Words with the short "Qq" sound:
quart, quote, quiet, quick, quality, quack, question, quiz, queen, quit

Self-Test:
1. Name the 4 steps to pronounce the long "Qq" sound.
2. Name 4 abbreviations or words with the long "Qq" sound.
3. Name the 4 steps to pronounce the short "Qq" sound.
4. Name 10 words with the short "Qq" sound.

Lesson 18:
The Long and Short Sounds of "Rr"

To pronounce the long "Rr" sound:
1. Place tongue against the middle of bottom teeth
2. Pronounce by Slightly open mouth
3. Bring lips to an oval position (lips in whistling position)
4. Bring mouth back to slightly open position (Step 2)
5. Ending position of tongue is at bottom of lower teeth

Abbreviations with the long "Rr" sound:
RV, R&R, RN, OR, IRS, DHR, PR, ER, MRI, HR

To pronounce the short "Rr" sound:
1. Place tongue against the middle of lower teeth
2. Pronounce by bring lips to a oval positions (lips in whistling position)
3. Bring mouth to slightly close position
4. Ending position of tongue is at bottom of lower teeth

Words with the short "Rr" sound:
race, rush, ran, road, red, rock, read, raw, rent, roll

Self-Test:
1. Name the 5 Steps to pronounce the long "Rr" sound.
2. Name 10 abbreviations with the long "Rr" sound.
3. Name the 4 steps to pronounce the short "Rr" sound.
4. Name 10 words with the short "Rr" sound.

Lesson 19:
The Long and Short Sounds of "Ss"

To pronounce the long "Ss" sound:
1. Place tongue against the middle of bottom teeth
2. Pronounce by slightly opening mouth
3. Spread lips apart (lips in smiling position)
4. Ending position of tongue is against the middle of lower teeth

Words with the long "Ss" sound:
essay, escort, estate, escape

To pronounce the short "Ss" sound:
1. Place tongue against the middle of bottom teeth
2. Pronounce by slightly opening mouth
3. Ending position of tongue is at bottom of mouth

Words with the short "Ss" sound:
sad, see, say, set, saw, sit, side, self, sand, six

Self-Test:
1. Name the 4 steps to pronounce the long "Ss" sound.
2. Name 4 words with the long "Ss" sound.
3. Name the 3 steps to pronounce the short "Ss" sound.
4. Name 10 words with the short "Ss" sound.

Lesson 20:
The Long and Short Sounds of "Tt"

To pronounce the long "Tt" sound:
1. Place tongue against top of mouth near upper teeth
2. Pronounce by Slightly spreading lips apart (lips in smiling position)
3. Slightly open mouth
4. Ending position of tongue is at bottom of lower teeth

Words with the long "Tt" sound:
teen, tee, tea, tease, teeth, tepee, teach, team,

To pronounce the short "Tt" sound:
1. Place tongue against top of mouth near upper teeth
2. Pronounce by opening mouth
3. Ending position of tongue is at bottom of lower teeth

Words with the short "Tt" sound:
tag, tan, tail, tall, talk, two, tie, tiny, tell, table

Self-Test:
1. Name the 4 steps to pronounce the long "Tt" sound.
2. Name 8 words with the long "Tt" sound.
3. Name the 3 steps to pronounce the short "Tt" sound.
4. Name 10 words with the short "Tt" sound.

Lesson 21:
The Long and Short Sounds of "Uu"

To Pronounce the long "Uu" sound:
1. Place tongue against the middle of lower teeth
2. Pronounce by slightly opening mouth
3. Bring lips to a slightly open position (extend lips outward)
4. Ending position of tongue is at bottom of lower teeth

Words with the long "Uu" sound:
you, united, unify, use, utopia, usual, unit, union, usage, unicorn

To pronounce the short "Uu" sound:
1. Place tongue against middle of bottom teeth
2. Pronounce by slightly opening mouth
3. Ending position of tongue is at bottom of lower teeth

Words with the short "Uu" sound:
up, ugly, upon, us, until, uncle, undo, utter, under, unless

Self-Test:
1. Name the 4 steps to pronounce the long "Uu" sound.
2. Name 10 words with the long "Uu" sound.
3. Name the 3 steps to pronounce the short "Uu" sound.
4. Name 10 words with the short "Uu" sound.

Lesson 22:
The Long and Short Sounds of "Vv"

To pronounce the long "Vv" sound:
1. Place tongue against the middle of lower teeth
2. Fold bottom lip over bottom teeth
3. Place top teeth on bottom lip
4. Pronounce by slightly opening mouth
5. Ending position of tongue is at bottom of lower teeth

Words with the long "Vv" sound:
veto, Venus, envy

To pronounce the short "Vv" sound:
1. Place tongue against the middle of lower teeth
2. Fold bottom lip over bottom teeth
3. Place top teeth on bottom lip
4. Pronounce by slightly opening mouth
5. Ending position of tongue is at bottom of lower teeth

Words with the short "Vv" sound:
vote, vary, vine, value, verb, visit, voice, very, vibe, van

Self-Test:
1. Name the 5 steps to pronounce the long "Vv" sound.
2. Name 3 words with the long "Vv" sound.
3. Name the 5 steps to pronounce the short "Vv" sound.
4. Name 10 words with the short "Vv" sound.

Lesson 23:
The Long and Short Sounds of "Ww"

To pronounce the long "Ww" sound:
1. Place tongue against top of mouth and near top teeth
2. Pronounce by slightly opening mouth
3. Place tongue at bottom of lower teeth
4. Place lips together
5. Slightly open mouth
6. Place lips in an oval position (extend lips outward)
7. Ending position of tongue in at bottom of lower teeth

Abbreviations with the long "Ww" sound:
P.O.W. (Prisoners of War), WWW (World Wide Web), WWI (World War I)

To pronounce the short "Ww" sound:
1. Place tongue against middle of lower teeth
2. Place lips in an oval position (extend lips outward)
3. Pronounce by slightly opening mouth
4. Ending position of tongue is at bottom of lower teeth

Words with the short "Ww" sound:
was, we, why, win, well, wet, walk, week, wall, want

Self-Test:
1. Name the 7 steps to pronounce the long "Ww" sound.
2. Name 3 abbreviations with the long "Ww" sound.
3. Name the 4 steps to pronounce the short "Ww" sound.
4. Name 10 words with the short "Ww" sound.

Lesson 24:
The Long and Other Sounds of "Xx"

To pronounce the long "Xx" sound:
1. Place tongue against the middle of bottom teeth
2. Pronounce by slightly opening mouth
3. Spread lips apart (lips in smiling position)
4. Ending position of tongue is against the middle of bottom teeth

Words with the long "Xx" sound:
x-ray, extra, export, exit, excuse, excess, example, exhale, expire, expand

Other sounds of "Xx":
"Xx" as the long sound of "Zz".
To pronounce, see *the long sound of "Zz"*

Words with "Xx" as the long sound of "Zz":
xebec, xenia, xenon

"Xx" as the short sound of "Zz":
To pronounce, see *the short sound of "Zz"*

Words with "Xx" as the short sound of "Zz":
Xylophone, xylem, xylograph

Self-Test:
1. Name the 4 steps to pronounce the long "Xx" sound.
2. Name 10 words with the long "Xx" sound.
3. Name 2 other sounds of "Xx".
4. Name the steps to pronounce "Xx" as The Long Sound of "Zz"
5. Name 3 words with "Xx" as The Long Sound of "Zz".
6. Name the steps to pronounce "Xx" as The Short Sound of "Zz".
7. Name 3 words with "Xx" as The Short Sound of "Zz".

Lesson 25:
The Long and Short Sounds of "Yy"

To pronounce the long "Yy" sound:
1. Place tongue against the middle of bottom teeth
2. Pronounce by extending lips outward
3. Slightly open mouth
4. Ending position of tongue is at bottom of mouth

Words with the long "Yy" sound:
why, Wyoming, Wyatt

To pronounce the short "Yy" sound:
1. Place tongue against the middle of bottom teeth
2. Pronounce by extending lips outward
3. Slightly open mouth
4. Ending position of tongue is at bottom of mouth

Words with the short "Yy" sound:
yard, young, yes, yet, yellow, you, youth, your, yours, yell

"Yy" sometimes as the long "Ee" sound:
baby, sunny, only, bunny, daddy, pony, donkey, skinny, party, lady,

"Yy" sometimes as the long "Ii" sound:
Cry, by, try, buy, fly, my, sly, spy, dry, unify

Self-Test:
1. Name 4 steps to pronounce the long "Yy" sound.
2. Name 3 words with the long "Yy" sound.
3. Name 4 steps to pronounce the short "Yy" sound.
4. Name 10 words with the short "Yy" sound.
5. Name 10 words with "Yy" sometimes as the long "Ee" sound.
6. Name 10 words with "Yy" sometimes as the long "Ii" sound.

Lesson 26:
The Long and Short Sounds of "Zz"

To pronounce the long "Zz" sound:
1. Place tongue against middle of bottom teeth
2. Pronounce by slightly spreading lips apart (lips in smiling position)
3. Slightly open mouth
4. Ending position of tongue is located at bottom of lower teeth

Words with the long "Zz" sound:
Zebra, lazy, zero

Long "Zz" sound of words that begin with "Xx":
xebec, xenia, xenon

To pronounce the short "Zz" sound:
1. Place tongue against middle of bottom teeth
2. Pronounce by slightly spreading lips apart (lips in smiling position)
3. Slightly open mouth
4. Ending position of tongue is at bottom of lower teeth

Words with the short "Zz" sound:
zoom, zone , zig-zag, zap

Short "Zz" sound of words that begin with "Xx":
Xylophone, xanthone, xylem

Self-Test:
1. Name 4 steps to pronounce the long "Zz" sound.
2. Name 3 words with the long "Zz" sound.
3. Name 3 words that begin with "Xx" and have the long "Zz" sound.
4. Name 4 steps to pronounce the short "Zz" sound.
5. Name 4 words with the short "Zz" sound.
6. Name 3 words that begin with "Xx" and have the short "Zz" sound.